# RUNNER'S HANDBOOK

## A HILARIOUS GUIDE TO SELF-ABUSE

# A HILARIOUS GUIDE TO SELF-ABUSE

## CRAIG TENNIS and
## MARTIN A. RAGAWAY

**PRICE/STERN/SLOAN**
*Publishers, Inc., Los Angeles*
**1984**

ISBN: 0-8431-7285-1

*There is a new breed of super-runners who push to their physical limits and beyond. To these marvelously motivated individuals, who find pleasure in heavy breathing (without getting emotionally involved), this book is respectfully dedicated.*

# TABLE OF CONTENTS:

# INTRODUCTION

A few years ago (in 1952 to be exact) the phrase "running around in circles" was used to describe senseless and erratic behavior. Today, it is a literal description of the country's very visible new aerobic-Religion.

The requirements for becoming a Born Again Runner are the same as those needed for any other Religion. All you have to do is Declare Yourself (and maybe buy a little equipment such as a Prayer Rug, an "I ♥ Jerry Falwell" button, a Yarmulke, a Crucifix or a pair of canvas shoes with rounded heels).

Running, like other religions, requires no special skills or talent, no intelligence, no particular physique—and it is uni-sexual.

It does require a certain brutal tenacity and a belief that Masochism can be Fun.

Historical precedents exist for this devotion to Self (you will pardon the expression) Abuse: The Medieval Flagellants, the Non-Recanting Victims of the Spanish Inquisition and Fans of the Chicago Cubs.

Today's Runner (the word "Jogger" is used only by owners of Royal Blue Warm-up suits that still have the original creases) runs, not to perfect his physical self, but as a means to Salvation. He runs as a penitent, to gain forgiveness for Being Alive.

But . . .

Given all of the above, it is still better to run than to spend that otherwise unused time watching television or eating carbohydrates. Running will in many cases strengthen the heart, revivify the lungs and intimidate the liver. And it makes you feel great. I know because I have been running for fifteen years. (My God, has it been that long since I lived on Central Park West?). In those days the only equipment needed was feet. But whether you are an old timer or a new timer, this book by Martin Ragaway and Craig Tennis will tell you a lot more about this invigorating form of ambulation than you really should know.

*Roger Price*

**Roger Price**
**February 8, 1984**

# RUNNING ISN'T FOR EVERYONE. IS IT FOR YOU?

Before you go out and spend money on running equipment you may never use more than once, you would be advised to answer honestly the following YES/NO questions:

**Can you sweat without making noise?**

**Do you have a *high* pain threshold?**

**Are you strong enough emotionally to whimper in public?**

**Can you talk to yourself while running, even though you know what an incredible bore you really are?**

**Can you place one foot in front of the other without consulting *The Arthur Murray Dance Book*?**

**Can you handle the indignity of having your neighbors saluting you as you run past by holding up their middle fingers?**

Are you aware that four out of five motorists actually believe they'll collect a bounty if they run you down?

Would you consider it a status symbol to have the ugliest feet on the block? Do you secretly enjoy maiming yourself? Could you learn to limp with pride?

Will you be upset if a dog says "hello" by lifting his hind leg?

Will your bed partner be sexually aroused by the fumes of Ben-Gay? Do *you* find Ben-Gay an aphrodesiac?

If you answered "yes" to any of the above questions, congratulations! You're a definite candidate for running!

# YOU KNOW YOU'RE IN BAD SHAPE WHEN . . .

Most human beings think they're healthy. But if you ask them why they think so, they'll ask *you* "Do I look sick?"

However, what most people fail to realize is that an absence of illness does not automatically mean good health. Some individuals hardly ever miss a day of work, but are in terrible physical condition. So before you assume you're healthy, ask yourself if you've recently encountered any of the following situations.

**No matter how much you hurry, you always get trapped in the middle of the intersection when the signal changes to "Don't Walk."**

**Burt Reynolds smiles and waves as he jogs by your house. Just waving back makes you so exhausted you have to lie down and take a nap.**

**Walking your dog makes you wheeze so loudly that cars pull over when their drivers hear you coming.**

The salesgirl at your local shoe store will only sell you jogging shoes if you promise not to tell anyone where you bought them.

You ran for the bus this morning and would have missed it if the lady expecting twins hadn't dashed ahead and held it for you.

You know so little about running you're willing to bet a week's salary that "Adidas" means "good-bye" in Portuguese.

You can't move fast enough to keep your pet turtle from running away.

When a mortician sees you shuffling out to the mailbox he gets out of his hearse to give you a business card.

Your girlfriend gets a snag in her panty hose, and you realize that the run on her leg is moving faster than you can.

You were so tired after seeing *Chariots of Fire*, the paramedics had to drive you home.

# HOW TO AVOID LOOKING
# LIKE A BEGINNER

You're taking up running, and it's important for you to look like you know what you're doing. There are two mistakes you can make.

ONE: YOU CAN USE YOUR OWN JUDGEMENT AND NOT SEEK ANY ADVICE

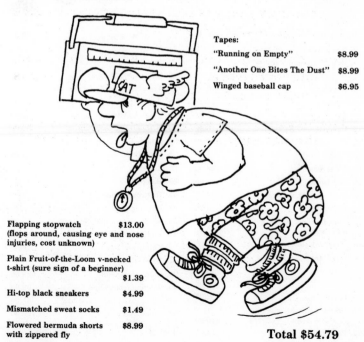

Tapes:

| | |
|---|---|
| "Running on Empty" | $8.99 |
| "Another One Bites The Dust" | $8.99 |
| Winged baseball cap | $6.95 |

Flapping stopwatch     $13.00
(flops around, causing eye and nose injuries, cost unknown)

Plain Fruit-of-the-Loom v-necked t-shirt (sure sign of a beginner)
    $1.39

Hi-top black sneakers     $4.99

Mismatched sweat socks     $1.49

Flowered bermuda shorts     $8.99
with zippered fly

**Total $54.79**

| | | |
|---|---|---|
| 1. PO2 Altitude Trainer | $219.00 | |
| 2. Designer ventilated tank top | 17.95 | |
| 3. Designer running shorts | 16.95 | |
| 4. Reflective vest for night running | 17.95 | |
| 5. Headband | 1.95 | |
| 6. Nosecote | 1.19 | |
| 7. Sony Walkman | 99.95 | |
| 8. Cassette tape *Rocky I* | 8.99 | |
| 9. Cassette tape *Chariots of Fire* | 8.99 | |
| 10. Chapstik | 1.19 | |
| 11. Pulse wand | 99.00 | |
| 12. Wristbands | 1.85 | |
| 13. Runner's I.D. dogtags | 6.95 | |
| 14. Rape whistle | 6.50 | |
| 15. Computerized digital gold wrist watch | 399.00 | |
| 16. Weighted gloves | 16.95 | |
| 17. Hand weights | 19.95 | |
| 18. Compass | 18.95 | |
| 19. Mace | 9.95 | |
| 20. Liquid Pak | 32.95 | |
| 21. Gore-tex running suit (2 pair of pants) | 215.00 | |
| 22. Pedometer | 14.95 | |
| 23. Ankle weights | 16.95 | |
| 24. Stretch laces | 2.69 | |
| 25. Key billfold | 3.65 | |
| 26. Short socks (3 pair) | 6.50 | |
| 27. Training shoes (custom-made) | 150.00 | |
| 28. Racing flats | 64.95 | |
| 29. Track spikes | 59.95 | |
| 30. Orthodics (prescribed) | 250.00 | |
| 31. Innersoles | 12.95 | |
| 32. Shoe-Goo | 3.95 | |
| Dietary aids: | | |
| 33. Bee pollen | 10.95 | |
| 34. Dextrose tablets | 4.99 | |
| 35. Running gum | .45 | |
| 36. Multi-vitamins (30 day supply) | 16.00 | |
| 37. Powdered ERG | .85 | |
| 38. Equipment bag | 15.95 | |
| Not Illustrated: | | |
| 39. Indoor treadmill | 699.00 | |
| 40. Jogging trampoline | 99.95 | |
| 41. Anti-gravity boots and bar | 81.90 | |
| 42. Home gym | 1,125.00 | |
| **Total** | **$3,862.74** | |

# THE SUPER-TRUTHS
# ABOUT RUNNING

Every sport is riddled with its own cliches: "Baseball is a game of inches," "You never know which way a football will bounce," and in basketball, "A good big man will always beat a good little man." The reason they became cliches is that they're true. Running is no exception: certain phenomena cannot be denied. These are the Super-Truths of running:

**The more expensive your running shoes, the sooner your dog will chew them up.**

**The further you plan to run in the morning, the more times you will be awakened in the middle of the night by wrong numbers.**

**No matter which direction you run on a blustery day, the wind will always be in your face.**

**Regardless of how bad you feel at the beginning of a run, you will feel even worse when it's over.**

Runners who claim they can't get enough interval training will also swear they never cheat on their spouses.

The more overweight a runner, the more likely he is to believe first person articles entitled "I Won The New York Marathon After Only 10 Miles of Training."

When you can no longer run to the top of a 3% grade, you may already be over the hill.

In the winter, when the sun is low in the sky, you're always freezing because the trees block out the warming rays of the sun. In the summer, when it sizzles, those same trees are of no help whatsoever.

The first time you've got yourself really primed to run 20 miles will be the day remembered as "The Surprise Spring Blizzard of '84."

Even though you run out and back on the same route each way, there will always be more uphill than down.

Running injuries occur only when you are at the farthest point away from home, and only when you don't have a dime for a telephone call.

If you still have sex on your mind during a hard training run, you aren't putting out enough.

# WHAT TO THINK ABOUT WHILE YOU RUN: FANTASIES TO HELP YOU FINISH

Those runners who are goal-oriented will continue to train even when the environmental elements are at their worst. A mere storm will not keep a dedicated runner indoors, and the determined ones deliberately seek out adverse conditions to make themselves mentally and physically stronger.

If you are working out in a stressful situation, you can alleviate some of the discomfort by externalizing your thoughts. Don't concentrate on what's hurting, but encourage your mind to relax with an unfocused stream of consciousness. Further, if you can create a heroic fantasy role for yourself, you'll hardly notice the miles as they speed by. And, if you can incorporate weather conditions into your personal scenario, so much the better.

The following fantasies are in public domain. You're entitled to use them without charge.

If it starts to RAIN—

... *What am I doing in the slimy, stinking, steaming tropical rainforests of Brazil? Why am I trying to save a tribe of Stone Age aborigines? Why me, Dr. Jonas Salk, Nobel Prize winner? Why am I drenched to the skin, when I could be warming my buns over a bunson burner back in my lab in La Jolla?*

... *Oh God! The storm washed out the bridge! Now when I reach the Amazon, I'll have to wade across. And, it's the widest part, too. 136 miles!*

... *I don't care about the quicksand or the leeches, but Lord, what will the piranha do to my new Nikes?*

If you're running and it's COLD—

*. . . What a spot! 25 degrees below zero, a wind chill factor of minus 80, and I've lost my mittens. Stupid of me to have worn white gloves in a blizzard.*

*. . . Perhaps I look familiar to you. You're right, I am Sergeant Preston of the Yukon, and I always find my man. But in a blizzard like this, if I wasn't wearing the proud red tunic of the Royal Canadian Mounted Police, I wouldn't be able to find myself.*

*. . . 200 miles north of the Arctic Circle, but I won't rest until I apprehend Pierre Duvall, the well-known Eskimo dog molester. And I'll take him alive . . . I'm so lonely. I hope he's a good conversationalist.*

*. . . I've been tracking this rotten, revolting, renegade for six months. I've dug myself out from under avalances, I've been trampled by herds of musk oxen. I've fought off three polar bears and slept with caribou! And for this, I am paid $76.00 a month. I wouldn't do it, if it wasn't such easy money.*

Runners know that HEAT is the most dangerous obstacle an athlete has to face. Heatstroke is insidious because by the time you're affected by it, it's too late to do anything—

*. . . A tenacious journalist will run down a hot story to the ends of the earth, and even further, if he must. And that's why yours truly, Henry Morgan Stanley, of the New York Herald (I'm sure you've*

*seen my byline), is here in the trackless wastes of the Southern Sudan. If there is a hell on earth, this must be the Devil's frying pan—a broiling, barren, baking, blistering desert of corrugated sand dunes.*

*. . . I am trailing a famous lost explorer, who set out to find the headwaters of the Nile. But I must push on, no matter what the cost. My tongue is black and swollen and hanging out of my mouth. It looks like I'm carrying a Samsonite attache case in my teeth.*

*. . . Ah ha, there's an oasis up ahead, and look, shimmering in the heat, a lone figure in a pith helmet.*

*. . . At last, now I can ask the question that will make me famous forever. "Dr. Livingston I Presume. Tell me, Dr. Presume, what does the 'I' in your name stand for?"*

Some serious runners who feel the need for altitude training often relocate to cities like Boulder, Colorado, or Taos, New Mexico, for that very purpose. Training at altitude is a very tough adjustment for a runner's respiratory system, because initially his blood stream has to struggle to absorb enough oxygen from the thin air—

*. . . I know what you're thinking, why is Sir Edmund Hillary, a man who climbed to the top of his profession, who's won fame and fortune, who was made a Knight of the Garter by the Queen— why is he risking everything on the treacherous slopes? I'm already as famous as I can be. Why am I climbing Mount Everest? Because I'm there and it's here.*

*. . . As long as you insist, I'll tell you why I kicked off my bunny slippers and donned a goosedown parka, and am once again at the 20,000 foot level of the world's highest mountain. I'm tracking the most elusive creature left on earth—the Abominable Snowperson. (I may be an intrepid explorer, but I'm no sexist.)*

*. . . If I have to keep this up much longer, my lungs will expand to the size of the Goodyear blimp.*

*. . . And the footprints I follow in the snow, spiral ever upward, around and around the peak. Oxygen deprivation is giving me hallucinations— for a moment there, I thought I was Rosie Ruiz.*

. . . *But once again, my logic is undiminished. As hard as it is to breathe, I must follow Yeti. Eventually he/she will lead me to the hidden crevice, which opens into the secret cave, which will guide me to the long lost tunnel, spilling out into the paradise—Shangri-la.*

. . . *Look at those footprints, it's either the Abominable Snowperson or somebody is running around in Kareem Abdul-Jabbar's sneakers.*

. . . *Wait, what do I have here? The secret passage, at last, I have found it!*

. . . *I guess I should check with that person at the front desk in the cashmere kimono.*

"*It's an honor to have you here with us at the Shangri-la Sheraton, Sir Edmund. Forgive me for asking, but how do you intend to pay for your accomodations while you're with us?*"

"*Gee, in the movie it was free . . .*"

"*Don't worry, we honor American Express.*"

Another advocational hazard for runners has a collar, four legs and an owner who swears, "I don't understand, he's never bitten anyone before." Dogs, who fondly lick the hands of cat burglars, become canine psychopaths when they think a runner is threatening their turf.

. . . *Fans of Mother Russia, Tovarich!*

*I know you recognize me from the Moscow Art Theatre. My name is Constantin Stanislavski, and there is a method to my madness.*

*. . . So what am I doing here in these icy woods, a thousand miles from the lights and thrills of downtown Moscow? I am helping Nicholas and Alexandra and their children escape from the Bolsheviks. I'd do anything for the Czar, Czarina and all the little Czardines.*

. . . When the wolves attacked us, I made the supreme sacrifice: I lightened the troika, jumping out so the horse-drawn sleigh could escape.

. . . Now the voracious timber wolves are pursuing me—I can feel their carnivorous breath right through these sable warm-ups.

. . . Oh good, some of the wolf pups are tiring and dropping back. Thank God, now there are only fifteen of the most vicious young males still trying to pull me down.

. . . Eighteen miles and I'm holding my own. There's only one still dogging me—a 200 pound, snarling, snapping, red-eyed, yellow-fanged mass of monster muscle.

. . . Opps, I just tripped over a couple of steppes, and he's got me! I'm on the ground, his vise-like jaws clamped around my throat!

. . . Maybe I can dazzle him with some party dogma. "Comrade Wolf, even though I'm a White Russian, I acknowledge that because of our glorious Revolution, there is freedom of speech, freedom of religion, and freedom from hunger."

. . . Look at that, he's released his death grip on my jugular and he's backing away in disgust! There are some things that even a Russian wolf won't swallow.

# DA AGONY OF DE FEET!

The foot is one of nature's most forgiving and durable creations. It must tolerate the restrictions of pointed shoes, cowboy boots and high heels. It's asked to kick the tires on used cars, punt footballs, and doesn't get any rest until you, yourself, kick off. Feet are susceptible to athlete's foot, bunions, warts, corns, blisters, calluses and only get noticed when they smell bad.

The foot is frequently rejected, neglected and left unprotected. And it shouldn't be—it's a masterpiece of evolutionary engineering. The foot has 26 individual bones, over 100 ligaments and a highly complex bio-mechanical system of tendons and muscles.

To better grasp the magnitude of the abuse it takes, consider this from Danny Schrier ...

*"When I run a marathon (26 miles, 385 yards), the length of my stride is approximately 36 inches or one yard. This means I must lift my body off the ground 46,145 times. And each time I put a foot down, it absorbs the equivalent of three times my body weight, which is 150 pounds, for a total weight of (body weight x 3) of 450 pounds. So over the course of a marathon, my feet must bear a total weight of (46,145 x 450), 20,765,000 pounds! This translates (divide by 2,000) to over 10,382 tons!!"*

If your stride is approximately one yard, over the course of a marathon, your feet will have to lift:

| YOUR WEIGHT | TONS |
| --- | --- |
| 100 | 6,922 |
| 110 | 7,614 |
| 120 | 8,306 |
| 130 | 8,998 |
| 140 | 9,609 |
| 150 | 10,382 |
| 160 | 11,075 |
| 170 | 11,767 |
| 180 | 12,459 |
| 190 | 13,151 |

# HOW TO UNDERSTAND INTERNATIONAL RUNNING SIGNS

In some communities, over-burdened police departments have been pressured into enforcing anti-running laws. The sight of someone running innocently down the street seems inexplicably to offend people who have no interest in running.

A small city in California tried to outlaw jogging until the ordinance was thrown out of the courts. But they didn't give up: they passed new laws restricting jogging to specific hours, and they made them stick.

In one Pennsylvania township, males are prohibited from running barechested and women aren't allowed to run in tanktops.

A retirement village in Florida permits runners to use the roads for training, but only if they run in single file.

In France, female runners have been the target of sexual harrassment, and none but the courageous still train.

So that runners can instantly recognize when they've entered a hostile community, warning signs have been standardized. We suggest you study these International Running Signs carefully so you will understand them and protect yourself accordingly—

DETOUR-PICNIC
IT IS ILLEGAL TO
SWEAT ON TUNA FISH
SANDWICHS.

BARBECUING OF
RUNNERS IN
DESIGNATED AREAS
ONLY

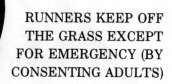

RUNNERS KEEP OFF
THE GRASS EXCEPT
FOR EMERGENCY (BY
CONSENTING ADULTS)

SHOOTING OF
RUNNERS BY
PERMIT ONLY

ALL DOGS MUST BE
CURBED ON THE
RUNNING PATH

RUNNERS ARE
FORBIDDEN FROM
ANNOYING PETS

RUNNERS
WELCOME

RUNNERS MUST
BE DRESSED
APPROPRIATELY

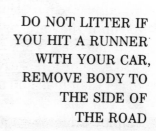

DO NOT LITTER IF
YOU HIT A RUNNER
WITH YOUR CAR,
REMOVE BODY TO
THE SIDE OF
THE ROAD

# OCCUPATIONS THAT CONFLICT WITH RUNNING

Some runners are fortunate to have jobs which do not interfere with their training, but actually complement it.

In fact, many corporations recently discovered that it is profitable to encourage running.

Not only do healthy employees take less sick leave, but they are also more productive and alert.

The company's health insurance rates drop and the expense of building showers and locker rooms quickly pays for itself.

Walt Disney Studios in Burbank, California, has known this for years, and its policy is to encourage its executives to participate in all sports, and to take time to run if they are so inclined.

When New York City was paralyzed by a transit strike, some innovative firms hired collegiate runners to get their mail and messages across town. It worked so well that now there are delivery services who employ athletes on a full-time basis.

The New York City Marathon was originally held entirely in Central Park, and one of the first winners managed to train while he worked. He was a Fuller Brush Man and he ran from door to door while he was training.

But if you have any of the following jobs, we advise caution: Running May Be Detrimental to Your Career . . .

## HOOKERS:

Streetwalkers should not run. by the time a potential customer catches up, he's so out of breath that he'll only be interested in going to bed by himself.

## LETTER CARRIERS:

Postmen should not run. In fact, whenever possible, tiptoeing is advisable. Why wake up more angry Dobermans than you have to? Also, a letter carrier who runs through his appointed rounds may commit the misdemeanor of delivering the mail on time, an offense which could cause immediate expulsion from the Postal Employees Union.

## WAITERS:

Restaurant personnel should absolutely not run, because they might get the food to the customer while it is still hot. Delicatessen waiters shouldn't even walk—they should continue to shuffle as they have done for centuries. A pastrami sandwich must be allowed to age. (If it gets from counter to the customer in less than fifteen minutes, it loses its ability to cause heartburn.)

## PROFESSIONAL FLASHERS:

While it is expected that streakers run, it is nonproductive for flashers. If exhibitionism is your thing, you want to be seen upclose and in person.

## POLICEMEN:

Cops shouldn't run after criminals because they might catch them. We already have enough of a problem with overcrowded prisons.

## FLOORWALKERS:

No one has ever seen a floorwalker in a hurry. The only people in department stores who rush around and seem to know what they're doing are shoplifters.

## EXECUTIVES:

Should not run after their secretaries. If she's a modern woman, she can fill out a sexual harrassment complaint without even breaking stride.

## POLITICIANS:

Shouldn't run, period.

# HOW TO TELL WHEN RUNNING IS RUNNING YOUR LIFE

Running is addictive. And if you're not careful, it can become the primary focus of your life. Everything will revolve around your daily workouts. Not only could this be destructive to your home life and your work at the office, but you're likely to become a bore at cocktail parties: when friends see you walk toward them, *they* run. You should know running has taken over if—

**Your lover leans over in bed, whispers, "How was it for you?" and you automatically respond, "It was okay, but it wasn't my Personal Best."**

**You can recognize the people you train with just by the sound of their footsteps.**

**You personally resent any car that uses the same street that you do.**

**Saks Fifth Avenue will not let you shop in your sweatsuit after a workout because you leave puddles.**

Your husband says, "Would you mind running this package over to the post office for me?" and you never consider taking the car.

Your idea of formal wear is white shorts, a white mesh singlet and a black headband.

You write an angry letter to Puma complaining that you only got 12,000 miles out of your last pair of training shoes.

You miss a day of running, and it causes you more guilt than forgetting your Mother's Birthday.

The bottom of your feet are so callused that when you run barefoot it sounds like flamenco dancing.

When someone asks, "How far is it from Los Angeles to Santa Barbara?" you immediately answer "For Alberto Salazar it's 15 hours, but for me, it's 23 and a half."

You start buying Dr. Johnson's Foot Soap Powder in economy 500 pound barrels.

The manager of your full-service bank gives you an ultimatum. "Stop doing stretching exercises while you're waiting in line, or we'll start bouncing your checks!"

Your closest friends won't join you for pizza and beer; they're annoyed because you can devour an extra-large pepperoni and a pitcher by yourself and still look under-nourished.

When you open the new *Playboy*, you ignore the centerfold and go straight to the article on Mary Decker.

Despite what your wife thinks, you can carry on a conversation about something other than running . . . as long as the listener is moving at the same pace you are.

You tell your long-suffering husband you won't tolerate smoking. And that he has to smoke his pipe out on the upstairs porch.

You won't let your pet cat sleep on the bed, because when it comes to oxygen, you won't share with anyone.

You stop seeing a new girlfriend because she never goes all the way . . . She always quits 24 miles into a marathon.

# HELPFUL HINTS: THE JOY OF PAIN

### KNOW YOUR SHOE

The more you know about your shoes, the better you'll run. The modern running flat is the end result of years of testing in the laboratory and on the road. So before you go out and spend a small fortune on shoes that may not be right for you, we recommend you study this cut-away so you'll recognize each part of the shoe.

### SOLE SURVIVORS

There are several good products on the market which are useful for extending the life of a running shoe. If you are forced to train on concrete, you've probably discovered that while your soles have worn through, your uppers are still comfortable and in good shape. These products are gooey synthetics which can be spread over a worn spot on the shoe sole, adding many miles of longevity to a well-broken in pair of training shoes.

However, we recommend that you not run until the gooey patch has had sufficient time to harden.

## WHAT EXPERT ADVICE
## SHOULD YOU TAKE?

Sooner or later, you may be tempted to get "expert" running advice. Most cities now have running clubs with coaches who will try to correct your flaws and build speed and endurance. Coaches basically come in two styles, (1) cruel and (2) tyrannical.

Study the following instructions to see which form of self-abuse makes you the most comfortable.

| COACH A'S PHILOSOPHY | COACH B'S PHILOSOPHY |
| --- | --- |
| No pain, no gain. | Do it 'til you puke. |
| Keep your chin up. | Keep your eyes on the ground. |
| Let your jaw hang slack. | Do not nose breathe. |
| Don't pivot your shoulders. | Let your shoulders relax. |
| Lift from your neck. | Lift from your chest. |
| Lean into it. | Don't bend from the hips. |
| Pump those arms. | Don't pump those arms. |
| Keep you arms parallel to the ground. | Pretend you're hitting someone in the stomach. |
| Rotate your thumbs up. | Rotate your palms in. |
| Relax those fists. | Pretend you're carrying live birds in your hands. |
| Lift those knees. | Don't lift your knees. You're wasting energy. |
| Lengthen your stride. | Shorten your stride. |
| Extend your legs. | Kick yourself in the butt. |
| Let your ankles float around. | Don't let your feet flop. |
| Land directly over your feet. | Stop taking chicken steps. |
| Land on your heels first. | Land on your midfoot. |

42

# THE FUNNIEST RUNNING STORIES YOU'VE NEVER RUN ACROSS

Larry and Frank had been running buddies for twenty years. One day over a beer, Larry wondered out loud if there was running in heaven. After a few more beers, they made a vow. The first who died would somehow get a message back to the survivor. Two months later Frank passed away, and for weeks Larry was inconsolable. Finally, he sought the services of a medium and attended a seance. Sure enough, the medium was able to produce an apparition of his buddy.

"Tell me, Frank, is there running in heaven?" Larry wanted to know.

"I have good news and bad news," the ghostly Frank replied. "The good news is that there's plenty of running in heaven. The bad news is that you're anchoring our relay team, starting tomorrow."

The finish line of any large road race is always somewhere between chaos and shambles. To scientifically sort out the finishing order, an inventor in Baltimore created a magnetic I.D. strip that can be inserted in the sole of a runner's shoe. Each strip gives off a different code as the individual runner crosses a photo-electric cell at the finish line. As each runner finishes the race his magnetic strip triggers a computer which then instantly prints out name, division, time and order of finish on a read-out of the race results. As the inventor explains, "These are the soles that time men's tries."

An Arabian sheik hired a top track star to be his personal assistant. When the sheik was in the mood, one of the young man's duties was to run from the Palace to the Harem, a distance of about three miles, to fetch one of the sheik's wives. This happened three to four times a day. The sheik would nod and the track star would take off. This arrangement went on until the runner died at the age of 42. The sheik lived to be 91. The moral of this story is, "Sex doesn't kill you, it's running after it that does."

God and the Archangel Gabriel were up in Heaven observing the finish of a 10-K race. Suddenly Gabriel noticed that even though it was Yom Kippur, the Jewish Day of Atonement, a Rabbi was running.

"That's terrible," said Gabriel, "he should be in Temple praying!"

"Don't worry," said God, "I'll make him suffer."

As Gabriel watched, the Rabbi, who had faltered, suddenly got a miraculous second wind and sprinted past the leaders, setting a new course record. Gabriel turned to God and said, "You call that punishment? Allowing him to win? And on Yom Kippur?"

God shrugged and said, "So who will he be able to tell?"

In a farming community, a woman was finishing a long workout on a hot, humid day, and was feeling particularly sweaty, dirty and unattractive. As she rounded a corner, another runner came toward her from the opposite direction. "Pig!" he wheezed. The woman found the strength to shout back over her shoulder, "Up yours, jack-ass!" The next thing she did was trip over a huge hog in the middle of the road.

An insurance executive would jog to his office in the morning, and jog back home at night. But the routine began to bore him. A friend suggested he find something to keep his mind occupied, like rolling a hoop as he ran the five miles to the office. Then at night he rolled it back again. One evening he walked out of the parking area to discover his hoop had been stolen. He called the police but they weren't very sympathetic.

"It's not important enough for us to file a report," said the policeman on the phone.

"That's easy for you to say," said the runner, "but how the hell am I going to get home?"

A man was running through a suburban neighborhood in New Orleans and saw a new tennis ball next to the curb. He scooped it up and since he had no pockets, he tucked it in his shorts. A few blocks later, a woman out picking up her newspaper openly stared at the bulge in his shorts.

Embarrassed, the runner explained, "Tennis ball."

"Oh, you poor dear," she said, "I have tennis elbow and I know how painful that can be!"

Some running expressions have become part of the vernacular. L.S.D., or "long slow distance," is recognized as a training program to avoid the potential injuries that come from running hard over lesser mileage. And "intervals" are workouts where various distances are repeated at different speeds. But if you don't understand these terms, it can be confusing.

Like the time Harry spotted his friend George in the park. "Doing L.S.D.?" he asked.

"No," replied George, "Intervals. I'd like to pick up some speed."

This was overheard by an old timer on a bench who shook his head and said, "I know what L.S.D. is and I know about speed—but intervals? Do you shoot it or snort it?"

Racing application forms are so simple to fill out that normally no one can screw them up. But when it comes to runners, nothing is foolproof. Take, for example, a racing application that was received for the Atlanta Peachtree. Next to the space marked SEX, a female runner had written, "Of course, but never the day of the race."

The bridegroom was as out of shape as he was naive and his bride was complaining. He went to his doctor who suggested that he take up running. He even outlined a program. 10 miles a day for 14 days. Two weeks later the doctor got a call from the exhausted runner. "Well," said the physician, "I'll bet your sex life is improved."

"Actually, Doc, I don't know."

"Have you been running 10 miles a day?"

"I have."

"Well, what does your wife think?"

"I don't know. She's in New York and I'm here in Delaware."

# PROPOSED LEGISLATION FOR THE PROTECTION OF RUNNERS

Runners have constitutional rights. In order to protect them, running clubs have finally organized to lobby for new legislation. If you are a serious runner, we encourage you to contact your local government officials and insist that the following propositions be placed on the ballot.

**Be it resolved: Any driver who deliberately swerves his vehicle for the sole purpose of frightening a runner, shall serve as the carpeting on the Queensboro Bridge during the New York City Marathon.**

**The enactment of an ordinance: Change stop lights at all intersections to RUN and DON'T RUN.**

**An amendment stipulating that anyone who chases after runners yelling "Hut, two, three, four!" shall be required to run the infiltration course at Parris Island— standing up.**

Scofflaws who intentionally race their dirt bikes on the few trails specifically designated for running, shall have the word "Harley" tattooed between their "Davidsons."

Be it resolved: Those who run at least twenty miles a week be granted a $5,000 tax credit, because their lungs filter out the pollution in the air, making it less lumpy for everyone else.

An ordinance drawn to prevent dogs from harrassing runners. Owners of said canine delinquents, if found guilty, will themselves be spayed or neutered.

An air emissions control statute which makes it mandatory for any car slowly preceding a runner to be fitted with an extension tube which will funnel the carbon monoxide from the exhaust pipe right back into the closed car.

Any person convicted of throwing a foreign substance from a moving vehicle at a helpless runner shall be punished by ten years at hard labor, or 4,000 miles of interval training, whichever comes first.

Legislation that would establish the entire state of Oregon as a no-smoking zone.

Anyone who willfully steals the last remaining toilet paper from a restroom customarily used by runners shall be the guest of honor at a beer bust and chili tasting, and shall be chained in a department store window for 24 hours, with absolutely no access to porcelain facilities.

Any male person who has to have a tilt-away steering wheel in order to wedge himself into his car shall be prohibited from ever appearing in a public eating place in an acrylic jogging suit.

Persons who jam used bubblegum into the spouts of public water fountains, if convicted, will be force-fed salted peanuts on the hottest day of the year. To alleviate their thirst, perpetrators will be allowed to lick an Angora cat.

Be it resolved: Cyclists who quietly pedal up behind a runner and then at the last second scream "Look out!" will be required to ride their vehicle without a seat.

# ARE YOU RUNNING TOO MUCH?
# 25 TELL-TALE SIGNS

Running is definitely healthy, but like everything else, with the possible exception of sex (or tax refunds), there can sometimes be too much of a good thing. Pushing yourself to do extra miles too soon will cause a negative physical reaction, and instead of making the runner stronger, will actually break him down. The warning symptoms of over-training include a sudden increase in the resting pulse rate, depression and crankiness, a need for much more sleep, and lethargy even when awake. You never really feel well, and as one infirmity disappears, another takes its place.

There are other ways to tell. You're running too much when—

**The Environmental Protection Agency will not let you bury your sweat socks at a toxic dump site.**

**You overhear a gorgeous guy in a singles bar say "I like to do it twice a day," and when you find out he's not talking about training, you're disappointed.**

You've become so skinny that no one notices you behind your necktie.

The only erotic experience you can immediately recall is spreading Vaseline on the inside of your thighs.

You're invited to a formal dinner party and the hostess specifically requests that you not bring your armpits.

You faint and the paramedics discover you've overdosed on Gatorade.

When you look at your feet, you can't remember when at least one of your toenails wasn't black.

In the middle of the night, you leap out of bed and sprint an 880 before you realize what you heard wasn't a starting gun, but a car backfiring.

When the first thing you notice about a member of the opposite sex is that he or she pronates.

After six months of training, your wife times your performance. The good news is that you're 30 seconds faster. The bad news is that she's referring to your sex life.

You find yourself wearing a running bra all the time, even with your strapless evening gown.

The only bumper sticker you will permit on your car is "Honk if you ♥ Mary Decker."

You divorce your husband and move in with your podiatrist.

You can tell your age by counting the rings of sweat in the crotch of your Dolphin shorts.

You have so many different 10-K shirts that you can run for three years without wearing the same one twice.

Dr. Scholl gets an injunction against your feet because you're giving his Odor-Eaters a bad name.

You can actually say "fartlek" in mixed company without giggling.

A beautiful woman says, "Hi, Big Guy, how can I make you happy?" And your immediate reply is, "Tell me how to break 40 minutes in a 10-K."

You actually look forward to birthdays so you can be eligible for a slower age group.

Your friends don't come to your house anymore, because if they want to smoke you make them sit inside a plastic laundry bag.

# SMALL TALK OR ITTY-BITTY INFORMATION (THE ONLY KIND REAL RUNNERS UNDERSTAND)

**WHAT MOTIVATES RUNNERS ...**
Siegfried Bauer once ran 1,000 miles in 12 days across the plains of South Africa. (It's amazing how far you can go when the runners behind you are carrying spears.)

**THE MYTH OF MYTHOLOGY ...**
Why is the marathon 26 miles, 385 yards long? Because that's the distance from Marathon to Athens, the distance run by the Greek messenger Phidippides? Wrong! The official marathon distance wasn't established until the 1908 Olympics in England. The Royal Princess wanted to watch the start of the race from the comfort of Windsor Castle, so the Olympics officials backed up the starting line 1.36 miles to accomodate her.

## DOES GETTING A SECOND WIND REALLY EXIST, OR IS IT JUST IMAGINATION?

For years doctors doubted athletes claims of a second wind, a sudden burst of unexplainable energy. But Abebe Bikila, perhaps the finest distance runner in history, helped to prove that it was an actual physical phenomenon. Bikila was carefully monitored during a marathon, and displayed dramatic physiological changes three miles into the race. Suddenly there was an abrupt drop in his pulse rate, breathing and blood pressure.

## HOW TO BLOW A LOT OF SHOE ENDORSEMENT MONEY . . .

Bikila, who was born and raised in Ethiopia, defied the rules when he competed in the 1960 Olympic Marathon in Rome. Bikila ran along the rough, irregular, blisteringly hot cobbled streets of the Via Appica Antica, easily winning the Gold Medal . . . barefooted!

## PHYSICIAN, HEAL THYSELF . . .

Dr. Terence Kavanaugh, director of a cardiac rehabilitation unit in Toronto, had eight of his post-coronary patients extend their weekly recovery runs to 50 miles. They all entered the Boston Marathon in 1973. Only Dr. Kavanaugh failed to finish the race.

## LET'S GET TO THE HEART OF IT . . .

The heart is a muscle that will eventually wear out. Every beat takes you closer to that great big track meet in the sky. If you're 20 years old with a resting pulse of 80 (about normal) and you start running, you can probably drop your heart rate down to 50 without a great deal of effort. By the time you're 70, you could have saved 788,400,000 unnecessary contractions of your heart muscle.

## AHH, THE JOY OF THE LONLINESS OF THE LONG DISTANCE RUNNER . . .

Dr. George Sheehan is a cardiologist/runner/writer, who at age 50 was able to run a 4:47.7 mile! Dr. Sheehan once waxed poetically, "The jogger-runner stops smoking, loses weight and develops a relaxed, playful approach toward the absurdities of everyday existence. Distance running, the addiction that cleans his arteries, also cleans his mind and soul." (George has a wife and 12 children—which must indicate that running 10 miles a day leaves you with a lot of energy.)

# PHYSICIAN'S FOOTNOTES: ANSWERS TO YOUR MEDICAL RUNNING QUESTIONS

*BY DR. MAURICE CARTILAGE*

Dr. Cartilage has devoted a lifetime to running. He has run from medical boards on six continents. He has eluded countless malpractice suits. Currently, he is catching his breath in San Vesco, Costa Rica, and can be reached in care of General Delivery. If you wish a personal medical opinion, send a self-addressed, stamped envelope to Dr. Cartilage. He won't answer your letter, but he will be very grateful for the unused stamp.

*Dear Dr. Cartilage,*
*Why does racing cause me to go to the bathroom more often than I normally do?*
*Signed,*
*Rear-In-Dire-Straits*

*Dear Dire-Rear,*
*You're problem is caused by competitive anxiety. Pick your races carefully, making sure the only restroom is at the finish line. It won't solve your dilemma, but it will give you a greater incentive to get there first.*

*Dear Doc,*
*The wear pattern on my shoe soles is very peculiar.*
*I use up the outside edge before the inside edge.*
*None of my running buddies can explain it to me.*
*Signed,*
*Tired-Of-Kissing-My-*
*Soles-Good-Bye*

*Dear Sole-Kisser,*
*It's possible you have Morton's foot, which occurs when the second toe is longer than the big toe. This can cause abnormal weight distribution when you run. It was first discovered in Flatbush, where it was known as Mortie's Foot. But when the syndrome went uptown, so did the name. There is no known cure for this, but you can make it work for you. Grow your other toenails extra long and clip your Morton's nail short. Not only will this correct your push-off, but you'll also be able to run barefooted on the beach and pick up gum wrappers.*

> *Dear Maurice,*
> *I train about 50 miles a week. For the last two months, I have found that my lower back is extremely sore when I get home.*
> *Signed,*
> *Back-Home-In-Indiana*

*Dear Back-Home,*
*You may be the victim of sciatica, a lower back problem caused by spinal misalignment and muscle imbalance. I have many patients who suffer from this, and they are easy to spot in a race. They arch their backs so much their butts sometimes finish two seconds behind. If you don't have the time for corrective exercise, I suggest you learn to run backwards. Not only is it easier for you to see who's gaining on you, but it's possible your ass could win by a nose.*

> Dear Maurice Cartilage,
> I always get blisters when I run.
> Signed,
> Tippy-Tippy-Toe

Dear Tippy,
Blisters can be caused by running on extremely hot surfaces, by wrinkled socks, or by shoes that don't fit properly. I assume these blisters are on your feet? If they are on your hands, it would seem to me that you are running incorrectly.

> Dear M. Cartilage,
> My name is Ted, and when I run more than three miles, I find my shirt rubs against me and irritates my nipples. What do you suggest?
> Signed,
> Titillated Ted in Toledo

Dear Titillated,
I recommend you smear petroleum jelly on your nipples and wear a looser T-shirt. If this doesn't work, wear Band-Aids, but this may cause a chest hair problem on removal.

*Dear Doctor,*
*When I finish my workouts, I notice my thighs have rubbed together and that I have chafed them raw. This causes two problems. Not only do I walk funny, but I have great difficulty explaining this condition to my boyfriend. What should I do?*
*Signed,*
*Miserable-Between-My-Legs*

*Dear Miserable,*
*Don't do anything rash. Your problem can be alleviated by changing your running form. Practice a new style. When you run, pretend you're straddling a low brick wall. If this doesn't work, you can reduce the friction by taping paper to the inside of your thighs. To pacify your boyfriend, write on the paper, "If you're close enough to read this, I love you!"*

*Dr. M. Cartilage,*
*When I finish a long run, I have sharp pain and swelling in the back of my ankles. It hurts so much I can't even walk up two flights of stairs to see my girlfriend.*
*Signed,*
*Stiff-Where-It-Doesn't-Do-Any-Good*

*Dear Stiff,*
*Considering the limited information you've given me, I'd say you're suffering from Achilles Tendonitis, an inflamation of the heel cord. To relieve this, I suggest a procedure which combines a double martini and keeping your foot on ice. The problem here is finding a martini glass large enough for your foot. You'll probably want to drink the martini later, so be sure to remove your New Balances and wash your feet.*

*Dear Dr. Cartilage,*
*A lot of runners I know put in extra miles because they think it will help them stay young. However, when I find myself halfway through a hilly 10-K, I pray for a bolt of lightning to kill me and put me out of my misery. What's wrong with my attitude? Signed,*
*Collapsed in Cleveland*

*Dear Collapsed,*
*You are permitting the physical aspects of the sport to overshadow the spiritual experience. The next time you're in agony, think how lucky you are: You have experienced Hell without dying.*

# NEVER USE THESE EXCUSES TO AVOID A WORKOUT

There will be days when you just don't feel like running. So you need an excuse that your running friends will believe, and more importantly, a lie even you can accept. Finding the right alibi is frequently more difficult than actually getting up, putting on your shoes, and just doing the damn run. However, if you insist on not running, you must avoid the hopelessly lame excuse. To keep your friends and loved ones from dismissing you as a candy-ass, never, never use the following for they have been laboratory tested and proven totally ineffective.

These Excuses Definitely Won't Work—

**"There's nothing I can do, I got up this morning and my feet were on the wrong legs."**

**"Last night I dreamed I ran in the Boston Marathon, so this morning I'm much too tired."**

**"My sweatglands have to go in for their 10,000 mile check-up."**

"Believe me, I'm dying to get out there with you, but I promised my wife I'd alphabetize her grocery store coupons."

"I shampooed my toes last night and I can't do a thing with them."

"Of course, I want to work out, but I'm having the shoelaces on my Etonics re-tipped."

"I know I said I'd train 15 miles this morning. but don't worry, I'll make it up by running 30 miles tomorrow."

"My foot fell asleep, and I can't wake it up. If it doesn't get at least eight hours, there's no living with it."

"Look, the inside of my thighs are so chafed, everything I move it sounds like a pair of corduroy pants calling its mate."

# HOW TO READ BETWEEN THE "LIES" OF A RACE APPLICATION

If you are entering an organized race for the first time, you are probably approaching it with a certain amount of apprehension. That's very intelligent. It indicates your fear is healthy and normal.

Get to the starting area early. You'll find the more experienced runners will gladly share their knowledge. The only people you can't trust are the ones who got you and your money there in the first place: The Race Promoters.

It's not easy to be a race promoter. It requires years of diligence and hard work, before a promoter can acquire the proper credentials. They learned their trade by selling 100-year lightbulbs, DeLorean franchises, bust developing kits, and vitamin E suppositories through the back pages of *The National Enquirer*.

## IF THE RACE APPLICATION SAYS—
"We know $12.00 seems like a large entry fee, but all the proceeds go to Good Guys for a Good Cause . . ."

## THE TRUTH IS:

## IF THE RACE APPLICATION SAYS—
"The Race will positively start at 8:00 AM . . ."

## THE TRUTH IS:

# IF THE RACE APPLICATION SAYS—
## "No one cares who wins, it's just a Fun-Run!..."

## THE TRUTH IS:

# IF THE RACE APPLICATION SAYS—
## "The course you will race on is gently rolling...

## THE TRUTH IS:

**IF THE RACE APPLICATION SAYS—**
   "This is a little community get-together. Your
   chance of winning is as good as anybody
   else's!"

**THE TRUTH IS:**

**IF THE RACE APPLICATION SAYS—**
   "Everyone will receive a beautiful trophy . . ."

**THE TRUTH IS:**

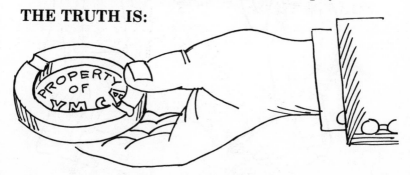

**IF THE RACE APPLICATION SAYS—**
"Aid Stations will
be provided every
three miles . . ."

**THE TRUTH IS:**

**IF THE RACE APPLICATION SAYS—**
"The results will be computerized . . .
**THE TRUTH IS:**

## IF THE RACE APPLICATION SAYS—
### "Deluxe transportation will be provided back to the starting area . . ."

## THE TRUTH IS:

## IF THE RACE APPLICATION SAYS—
### "Emergency Medical Care will be readily available . . ."

## THE TRUTH IS:

## IF THE RACE APPLICATION SAYS—
"We've held the Race in the same place for the last nine years because the temperature never gets above 60 degrees . . ."

## THE TRUTH IS:

## DIDN'T FINISH . . . SO NO FREE T-SHIRT!

## IF THE RACE APPLICATION SAYS—
"There will be plenty of toilet facilities at the starting line . . ."

## THE TRUTH IS:

## IF THE RACE APPLICATION SAYS—
"At the completion of the race, everyone is invited to a Gala Six-Course Victory Dinner . . ."

## THE TRUTH IS:

# WHEN IT COMES TO RUNNING, FACT IS STRANGER THAN FRICTION . . .

Harvey was a dedicated runner. The fact that he was also an engineer at a convention in San Diego did not prevent him from doing his regular ten miles a day. As he was leaving the Del Coronado Hotel, Jennifer, a very attractive blonde in running clothes, asked if she could join him. He was glad to have company and even though she had never done the distance before, he persuaded her to finish with him. She was exhausted but a good sport.

The next day Harvey was joined by his wife who flew down for the weekend. As they were riding down in the elevator, his running partner of the previous evening got in. "Good morning, Jennifer," he said, "I hope you recovered."

Jennifer said, "Thanks to you, I'm still sore."

That was four years ago and Harvey is still explaining it to his wife.

Herb Kummel was the owner of a boy's camp in Vermont, but he let nothing get in the way of his nightly workout, not even the end-of-the-season variety show. The dramatic counselor prevailed on him by saying, "Look, we need somebody like you for the blackout of the George Washington sketch. It'll only take a few minutes and you can do it while wearing your jogging outfit."

The owner thought for a moment and reluctantly agreed, "Well, in that case, I'll do it."

Herb's part was to run around the counselor who played the tree while the young George Washington was cutting it down. Herb ran, the tree fell and walked off the stage while Herb kept jogging in a circle.

Little George Washington turned to the assembled campers and said "I can not tell a lie. Even when the tree is gone, the sap keeps running."


Laszlo Tabori, the third man in the world to break the 4:00 mile, now coaches the San Fernando Valley Track Club in Los Angeles. To finish a Tabori workout requires not only speed and endurance, but it also helps to have an analytical, imaginative mind. He once told a world class runner "No more I want crooked foots! Do right, or get out of my eyes!" Translation from pidgin Hungarian: "Stop pointing your toes or I don't want to see you on the track anymore!"

In Monterey, California, Larry Weinreb makes a habit of running out to the lighthouse at the end of the peninsula. One morning he paused to do some Achilles stretching. Feet flat on the ground, legs quivering, he pushed hard against the base of the lighthouse. An old fisherman observed this for a moment, looked up from his rod and said, "Young fella, you push that thing over and ain't no one gonna be able to find the entrance channel."

Kevin Johnson, who runs in Atlanta, has been bitten several times by man's best friend (and the runner's worst). So he has taken to carrying a jogging baton for protection. During a run one day, he passed a driveway and was greeted by a ferocious looking German shepherd. As he turned to see if the dog was following him, he tripped. The dog looked as if he was going to attack so Kevin took his stick and hurled it at the dog. The baton twirled over the canine's head and Kevin leaped to his feet and ran as fast as he could. The dog came after him and followed him right onto his front porch. As he prepared to defend himself, the dog, panting hard and wagging its tail, dropped the stick at his feet.

Arthur Lydiard, the noted running coach and speaker, is frequently asked the following question, "How do you determine the best event for a runner?"

Lydiard's reply is, "I hold a candle up to their ears. If light comes out the other side, I know they're perfect for long distance running."

Inclement weather always reminds veteran runners of a famous incident that happened during the Falmouth Road Race. Two close friends were halfway through the course when the sky suddenly opened and a deluge of rain fell on them. Struggling just to see, they slogged onward until a bolt of lightning struck a tree just yards away. When they stopped sprinting and the adrenalin rush allowed them to speak again, one gasped to the other, "I think I just peed in my pants . . . but I can't tell."

It was John's first marathon in Boston. He had run 20 miles and was about to hit the wall when he spotted a public phone booth up ahead. A runner was using the phone and John thought he was calling a friend to pick him up. Instead, the runner dashed out of the booth and took off with a new burst of energy. As John reached the booth, the phone was ringing. Curious, John answered the phone and heard a voice say, "For God's sake, don't quit now!" It was just the encouragement John needed. He hung up and took off. As he did, he could hear the phone ringing again.

# ABSOLUTELY INCONTROVERTIBLE FACTS ABOUT RACING

There are many therapeutic reasons for running. It's great for the cardiovascular system. Under the proper conditions, it's as mentally relaxing as transcendental meditation. It gives men and women confidence and a sense of accomplishment that cannot be found in most other recreation. And even as they surrender to fatigue, they feel new respect for themselves.

For many runners, racing is the icing on the cake. While training, they were competing only against themselves. But the only way to find out how good they really are is to enter a race where there are apt to be hundreds or thousands of equally dedicated competitors.

For serious runners, it's the moment of truth:

Have they enough discipline to pace themselves correctly?

Has their training regime been effective?

Have they the courage to gut it out when their bodies want to quit?

Racing is the oldest form of sports competition known to humans. From the moment a caveman said, "I can beat you to that tree and back," certain facts about racing were incontrovertible—

When a 10-K is incorrectly measured, it is never measured short.

The elastic in your shorts will not break until you're directly in front of the television cameras. (And it'll be the first time in years anyone has pronounced your name correctly.)

In a 26.2 mile marathon, the first 20 miles drains 80 percent of your strength; the last six miles takes 90 percent of your will power. So unless you can come up with 170 percent, stay home!

No matter how well you do in a race, your best friend, who's ten years older, will finish seven minutes ahead of you.

If you catch only one head cold a year, you will get it three days before the big race.

When there are prizes for the first 15 finishers, you will come in sixteenth.

If your shoelace breaks, it will happen 30 seconds before the starting gun goes off.

The runner you finally overtake 10 yards before the finish line always turns out to be a former cardiac patient wearing a T-shirt which says "I Participated In The Grandfather Games."

The best looking, sexiest hunk in the race is only there to meet other guys.

If you guzzle water at an aid station, every drop goes smoothly down your throat. If you drink Gatorade or ERG, it will spill and you'll be sticky for the rest of the race. And 600 excited bees will finish at the same time you do.

If it's the fastest race you'll run in your life, the official timing devices will malfunction.

# "I WOULD HAVE WON THE RACE, EXCEPT . . ."

Competition requires some fundamental preparation. The night before the race, the runner carefully examines his or her racing equipment and packs a ditty bag with such items as extra shoelaces, safety pins, Vaseline, warm-ups, etc. It's also advisable to drive or walk the course so the runner is familiar with the terrain.

On race day, the runner should arrive at the starting line with plenty of time to spare. This permits a normal routine of stretching exercises, and to run just enough to break sweat. Having taken care of the basics, the runner must set aside time for something really important—stockpiling believable alibis, so when people ask "How did you do?" the runner can say with no hesitation:

I Would Have Won The Race, Except—

**ALIBI . . .**
   "I was suffering
   from exposure."

**ALIBI . . .**
   "The girl who was pacing me sprinted
   near the finish line. It was all I could do to
   hang in there . . ."

**ALIBI . . .**
   "I got a late start . . ."

**ALIBI . . .**
   "I had to run for my life from a pack of killer dogs!"

**ALIBI...**

"My legs are shot. But what can you expect when sex keeps you awake all night?"

**ALIBI...**

"I got stuck at a railroad crossing..."

ALIBI . . .
    "I hit the wall at
    22 miles . . ."

ALIBI . . .
    "You didn't tell me it was an obstacle
    course. It's a jungle out there!"

**ALIBI . . .**

"Blame it on my mother. I was brought up believing 'Ladies Go First.'"

# THE WIT AND LACK OF WISDOM IN RUNNING

Having a pained expression does not make you run faster. So if you're having one of those great days and feel terrific, feel free to notify your face.

Don't be envious of athletes who have natural talent. Be grateful for the things they have but you don't: tendonitis, heel spurs, stress fractures and groin pulls.

An exhausted jogger can detect an uphill grade so insignificant that it would be missed by most surveyors.

Someone up there is telling you to go back to bed when you hit the wall during your stretching exercises.

Girl's running shorts seem to come in three sizes ... Small, Smaller and "Keep your eye on the road, Arthur!"

Running is merely putting one foot in front of the other. A world record is just repeating it often and fast enough.

Bill Rodgers, Frank Shorter and Marty Liquori are pure amateur athletes because they've never made a cent from running . . . and if you believe that, you also believe Dolly Parton sleeps on her stomach.

Nothing enrages a motorist as much as the sight of a vertical runner.

Making love burns just as many calories as running a mile, but running is healthier than sex. When you're through running, you don't crave a cigarette.

People who jog to work may not be dedicated athletes. It is possible the closest parking to their office is in their own driveway.

The late Pete Waters, a famous running coach, believed in one credo: "Any race you can walk away from is a bad race."

# YOU'RE NEVER TOO OLD
# TO GET IT ON . . .

The world record holder for the 50-and-over age division in the women's marathon is 54-year-old Sister Marian Irvine of San Rafael, California, who finished in 2:51:01. She is also the oldest person to qualify for the Olympic Marathon Trials! (Who says a habit isn't running forming?)

Friedrich Tempel began running at 65, and ran a 3:15:54 marathon at the age of seventy!

Paul Richel began running when he was 50. Ten years later he ran six sub- 3:30 marathons in less than 8 weeks—not to set a record, which it was, but simply as part of his normal workout!

Jack Foster of New Zealand didn't take up running until he was 32. He set a world record for 20 miles at the age of 39. At 41, he ran a 2:11:18 marathon, good enough for second place in the Commonwealth Games!

# THE MOST DIFFICULT DECISION: HOW TO QUIT RUNNING WITHOUT FEELING GUILTY

You are a local legend—the neighborhood guru of running.

For years, you've been acclaimed as an Ambassador of Sweat.

You have successfully harrassed all your friends into good health.

But sooner or later, there may come a time when you no longer want to run.

Ever again.

You're burned out, a puddle of permanent pain.

You have to quit—but it's not that easy.

When you announce that you're going to hang up the old Converses all your proteges will form a mob in front of your house and hang you by a part of your anatomy that was never intended to support weight. It isn't enough to just quit. You must go out in a blaze of sympathy.

Here are some time-tested techniques that will permit you to gracefully withdraw from the sport—

There are still a few doctors who think running is harmful. Keep switching physicians until you find one who will order you to quit.

Tell your friends, "Running is no longer a challenge, I'm into distance swimming now. Every morning I swim five miles at the lake. I can hardly wait for April, so I won't have to swim under the ice anymore."

"My husband threatened to leave me if I didn't give up running. For years I ignored him. Last week he split and now that he's gone there's no reason for me to keep running."

Plant a garden with only goldenrod, timothy grass and ragweed. If allergies make your nose run, you don't have to.

"I'm into cross-country skiing these days. And the first country I'm going to cross is Russia."

"I'll be in the hospital for major surgery . . . I'm having my sweatglands stitched closed."

"I had to quit because of my psychiatrist. She said, 'How long can you keep running away from your problems?' "

# THE RUNNER'S PRAYER

*Dear Lord, in thy Wisdom and Divine Mercy, grant me, thy humble servant, a simple miracle. With Your Blessing, may I arrive at the starting line of a race offering many rewards to its winners, and lo and behold, find I am the only runner in my age division.*
*Amen.*

# THE RUNNER'S HANDBOOK, PART TWO

is in preparation. We're also working on Part Three and Part Four. And we'll stay with it until we get it right.

We welcome your participation. Please send us your favorite running jokes, observations, cartoon ideas, or funny anecdotes:

THE RUNNER'S HANDBOOK
8625 Holloway Drive
Los Angeles, CA.
90069

If your suggestion is printed and is the first of its kind to arrive, you will receive credit (which will make you internationally famous), a free autographed book and a specially created T-shirt.* Be an optimist include your T-shirt size (S, M, L, XL) with your entry. Everything you send, of course, cannot be acknowledged (unless deemed publishable, as above) and is ours to do with as we see fit (see above).

*Unlike T-shirts awarded at most races, this designer apparel is guaranteed not to fade, unravel or shrink. However, if you wash this shirt, the warranty is no longer in effect.